MTN. VIEW HIGH MEDIA CENTER
DISCARDED

D1774723

M.V.H.S. MEDIA CENTER
CLASSIFICATION 92
            B)26
ACQUISITION #   6777

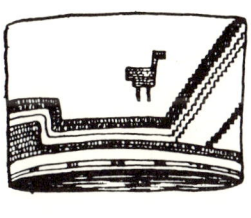

SEALTH

By Mel Boring

DILLON PRESS, INC.
MINNEAPOLIS, MINNESOTA

©1978 by Dillon Press, Inc. All rights reserved
Second printing 1980

Dillon Press, Inc., 500 South Third Street
Minneapolis, Minnesota 55415

Printed in the United States of America

Library of Congress Cataloging in Publication Data

Boring, Mel, 1939-
  Sealth.

  SUMMARY: A biography of the Indian chief, leader of the tribes of the Puget Sound area in the first half of the nineteenth century.
  1. Seattle, Chief of the Suquamish and allied tribes, d. 1866—Juvenile literature.
  2. Suquamish Indians—Biography—Juvenile literature. [1. Seattle, Chief of the Suquamish and allied tribes, d. 1866. 2. Suquamish Indians—Biography. 3. Indians of North America—Biography. I. Title.
E99.S85B67   970'.004'97 [B]   77-25470
ISBN 0-87518-155-4

The photographs are reproduced through the courtesy of the American Museum of Natural History; Minneapolis Public Library Athenaeum; Museum of the American Indian; National Museum of Canada; Public Archives of Canada; Seattle Historical Society; University of Washington Library; U.S. Department of the Interior, National Park Service; Washington State Department of Commerce and Economic Development; and the Washington State Historical Society.

ON THE COVER:
A portrait bust of Sealth, sculpted by James Wehn, that was placed in Pioneer Square in Seattle in 1909.

SEALTH

At the time the first European explorers came to Puget Sound in 1792, Sealth was a Squamish Indian boy of seven. Vancouver's visit left a lasting impression on young Sealth. Throughout his life, first as a Squamish chief and later as the leader of the allied tribes of the Puget Sound area, Sealth would have to deal with the whites and their desire for the land of his people.

Chief Sealth did all he could to live in peace with the white people. But when the Washington Territory was formed, the whites came in greater numbers and began to take the land of the Puget Sound tribes. Deprived of their homeland, Sealth's people could not feed or clothe themselves, and many starved. Sealth died in 1866, and with him died his dream of uniting the Indian and white worlds in peace.

Contents

I   THE WINGED SPIRIT page 1

II   THE GIANT CANOE page 9

III   WEDDING AT OLD-MAN-HOUSE page 14

IV   CHIEF SEALTH page 19

V   SEALTH THE PEACEMAKER page 26

VI   THE BOSTONS ARRIVE page 31

VII   SEATTLE page 37

VIII   DAY AND NIGHT CAN NOT DWELL TOGETHER page 44

IX   WAR page 51

X   A CHANGE OF WORLDS page 55

CHAPTER I

The Winged Spirit

The blustery March wind chilled the barefoot, copper-skinned boy. Twelve-year-old Sealth stole along the edge of the sound he knew as the Whulge. In the white world that was soon to be carved out of Sealth's world, it was known as Puget Sound.

The sound was a stout arm of the Pacific Ocean that twisted its way into the northwest corner of the land the white people would call the state of Washington. But now, in 1798, it was still the world of Sealth's people, the Squamish Indians.

The thickly needled branches of towering pines loudened the wind's howl. Cedar, fir, and madrona stood like warriors, guarding the slopes to *Puakooke*, the Mountain-that-was-God. The white people would call it Mount Ranier.

Sealth was cold and wet and hungry. But he wouldn't give up his search. His breechcloth flapped in the wind, which whipped the Whulge waters into a fury. The wind-hurled spray stabbed Sealth's body like icicle slivers.

He seized the biggest rock his arms could lift. The icy water numbed his legs as he wrestled the boulder out to his raft. He would use it to sink himself to the bottom, where he hoped to find what he was looking for.

To young Sealth, this was the Mountain-that-was-God. The white people would call it Mount Ranier.

3 THE WINGED SPIRIT

Clutching the rock, he stepped to the edge of the raft. The breath clouds disappeared at his lips as he drew in one final supply of air. He plunged into the freezing water, and the heavy rock dragged him down, down, till his breath beat like a deer's legs against his lungs.

Sealth didn't find what he was seeking at the bottom of the Whulge. So he let the rock go and pulled himself up the cedar bark rope to his raft. As soon as his nose cleared the surface, he gasped a fresh breath.

Once rested, he sloshed to the water's edge and quickly dried his shivering body with handfuls of pine needles. Then he started up the stony beach.

He hadn't eaten in days, but he had to go without food. If he didn't fast, his guardian spirit would not come to him. And he must bathe often in the cold waters of the sound. There was no other way.

That night Sealth built a fire and sat down to think. Finally he drifted off to sleep, unblanketed against the raw night winds. The spirits were more likely to come in foul weather.

Sealth hadn't found his guardian spirit that day. His father, Chief Schweabe, had said that it would come to him if he showed no fear of the forest or waters. And if he didn't shrink back from the hunger pangs in his stomach.

It might be found, Schweabe had told him, in the deep darkness of the tangled forest, or in the cold, dark waters of the Whulge. If he found it, Sealth's guardian spirit would protect him all through life.

All twelve-year-old Squamish boys sought their guardian spirit. But powerful spirits came only to those who endured many hardships. Sealth would not return to the Squamish village until he found his own.

Early the next morning he continued his search. After an ice water bath in the Whulge, he found an even bigger rock than the day before. Struggling out to the raft with it, he sucked in his breath and dropped, rock and all, into the water.

The boulder shot him downward like a yew-wood bow sends an arrow. Sealth's heart pounded in his ears. His lungs felt afire, ready to burst. Little by little he numbed to every feeling. The last thing he remembered was the salty tang of the Whulge water as it found its way into his mouth. The rock slipped from his sluggish arms. He floated upward.

A shrill screech woke Sealth. He was back on the beach, but he could not remember how he'd gotten there. Rocks were gouging his back. He opened his eyes.

The screechy sound came from a sea gull that soared low overhead. Sealth's senses began to clear. The pearl gray, feathered body floated motionless in the air. He cleared his eyes and peered at the gull hovering above him.

Sealth had found his guardian spirit—the sea gull. He ran for the Squamish village as sunset turned *Towiat,* the Olympic Mountains, a deep purple.

Sealth's mother, Scholitza, must have sensed he would be coming home that evening. She stood beside her blazing cooking fire.

Sealth entered the family home, a cedar-pole frame covered with mats of woven grass. The many-holed roof dripped rain into a steaming pot of salmonberry soup. The pot was a watertight basket, woven of reeds. Several hot stones were put in the bottom to heat the soup.

"Biscuits" of dried, ground fern roots baked near the hot coals. The sweet smell of dried blackberry cakes

Sealth's home looked much like this Salish dwelling. His mother may have been dressed in the clothes worn by these women of the Puget Sound region.

tempted the hungry young man, as well as smoked salmon, the main food of the Squamish. It had been smoked and dried the season before.

Chief Schweabe stood in proud silence beside Sealth. At more than six feet tall, he was a giant among the short, squatty, pigeon-toed Squamish. He had come from a long line of chieftains. The son he watched with quiet pride would someday grow to almost six feet himself.

Sealth tried to calm his hunger pangs while Scholitza prepared the meal. A proud, queenly woman, she was a Duwamish Indian, a tribe that lived across the Whulge toward the east.

Schweabe had hoped to rule the Duwamish as well as his own people. That was one reason he had married Scholitza. Slowly, however, he had begun to realize that his hopes would be fulfilled only in his son.

The Squamish were part of the larger Salish family of Indians who had long lived in southwest Canada and the northwest United States. When the interior of this land could no longer support the growing population, many Salish had migrated to the Pacific Coast.

Thousands of years before, Sealth's Squamish ancestors had made their way westward along the rivers and mountain passes that led to the coast. The Squamish had settled around Puget Sound. Their new world was separated from the interior by *Squacooke,* the Cascade Mountain Range.

Using the waters of the Whulge became a way of life to the Squamish. Their new world had over four hundred miles of bays, inlets, and tidal flats which they traveled in their cedar dugout canoes. They were called "canoe Indians" by their "horse Indian" relatives inland.

The Cascade Mountain Range rises to the east of the Whulge. Long ago the Squamish crossed these mountains on their way to Northwest Coast.

The Squamish ate fish and other seafood, such as smelt, herring, clams, cod, and their favorite, salmon. The meat of deer, elk, and beaver added to their rich diet. Ducks, geese, and pheasant flew into their traps.

The world of the Squamish was also rich in berries and roots. Salmonberries, gooseberries, and raspberries grew wild in the meadows. Roots like *wappatoes,* which were round, red, egg-sized potatoes, were dug by Squamish women. Wild onions and carrots grew in many places.

The coastal tribes' food-rich land gave them an easier living than the harsh climate of their inland Salish relatives. Over many hundreds of years, they had developed a more comfortable way of life. Many coastal tribes were noted for their wealth. They traded much among themselves, and they held feasts, called "potlatches," in which many gifts were given away.

Their rich land clothed the Squamish, too. The long skirt and simple shirt that Scholitza wore were made of cedar bark. Schweabe's fur cape and leggings kept out the cold of March. In summer, he would wear only a loincloth. To keep off the frequent rain, the Squamish wove cone-shaped hats of reeds and grass.

The simple clothes bore designs of paint, beads, and bone. Some Squamish men pierced the septums of their noses and decorated them with wood or shells.

With the coming of the white people, the world of the Squamish would go through great changes. But for now, Sealth and his family ate, dressed, and lived much as their ancestors had for thousands of years.

CHAPTER II

The Giant Canoe

Sea gulls soared high above Blake Island, where Sealth was born about 1786. Mile-wide Blake Island, now called Trimble, lies a mile or two south of the larger Bainbridge Island in Puget Sound. Bainbridge was the center of the Squamish world during Sealth's childhood.

The first white people had come to the Pacific Northwest long before Sealth was born. They were Russian fur traders, who arrived there in the early 1700s. In the last half of that century, Spanish sailors and English and American sea-otter traders came to the coast. But until the late 1700s, no white people had come to Squamish lands.

The British captain, George Vancouver, was the first to sail into the Whulge, which he named Puget Sound. Seven-year-old Sealth saw Vancouver in 1792, during the captain's three-week exploration of the Whulge. For Vancouver and his crew of the ship *Discovery,* it was a routine meeting like those they had had with many other Indian tribes. For the Squamish, however, it was their first encounter with the strange world of the white people.

On a misty May morning, the Squamish were camped at Bean's Point, near the south end of Bainbridge Island. Sud-

Sealth was born on this island in Puget Sound almost 200 years ago. In the background is Mount Ranier.

denly a huge ship loomed up out of the fog. For a moment, the Squamish stared at the strange sight. Then the people began to move toward the trees that skirted the beach. Fathers shouted orders. Mothers herded their children. Surprise attacks from warlike northern tribes had taught them to flee. Perhaps this was a Haida canoe!

Young Sealth didn't know whether to stand still or run. He looked from Schweabe to Scholitza. They were standing calmly, watching the strange craft.

Kitsap, the Squamish war chief, also stood his ground. He told the Squamish that these were the white people foretold by their ancestors. Squamish legends said white people would come on giant canoes, with masts as tall as fir trees.

Stories of the white people's arrival had spread among American Indians, from east to west across the land, ever since Columbus's landing three hundred years before. The Squamish decided to trust Vancouver's welcome and visit the *Discovery*.

Next morning, the Squamish killed a deer to give to the English explorers. They dressed it and added onions and berries to the gift.

Sealth squeezed into one of the canoes that carried eighty Squamish out to the *Discovery*. When they neared the ship, the canoes swung into a wide circle around it. The Squamish sang their tribal songs, keeping rhythm on the canoes with their paddles.

At Vancouver's first call, Sealth and the other Squamish clambered up the side of the ship. The young boy watched in wonder as Schweabe spoke to the white people in sign language and a few Squamish words.

And there were **things**—so many strange things on board

The Squamish were surprised by the great size of Vancouver's ship, the Discovery. *Another English ship also explored the Whulge.*

the canoe. The chains, knives, and muskets were the first metal objects he had ever seen. He saw metal forks and iron cooking kettles, and he watched as the sailors waved their shiny swords. They offered the Squamish a treat Sealth ate with delight—bread and molasses!

Vancouver issued orders in a crisp, commanding voice. What he told the white men, they did at once. The Squamish were surprised. Their own people talked much among themselves before taking action. First, everyone had to agree on what should be done.

When the trading began, the Squamish presented their deer to Vancouver. In return, he gave them a square-foot sheet of copper. The Squamish prized the bright orange metal above all the gifts because it could be made into any shape without breaking. They used it to make shields.

Vancouver was young, poised, and well built. With friendly, blue-gray eyes and a warm smile, he eased the fears of the Squamish. His kindness reached across the distance between them. It was a kindness, however, born of a misplaced pride. In his diary, he said of the wealthy, powerful tribe, "Today I met a rude, humble people. About five hundred on a whole island. Scarcely better than animals."

So the Squamish met with the forceful nature of the white people. Soon these two ways of life would clash, as the whites closed in upon the Indians in the Northwest. But young Sealth knew nothing yet of such differences. He only knew that he had touched and tasted the white world, and it seemed good.

CHAPTER III

Wedding at Old-Man-House

When Vancouver left in late May of 1792, it was time for the Squamish to gather their winter food supply. To do this, they would have to make three long journeys.

On the first food-gathering trip, the Squamish dug clams and other shellfish. They dug along the inlets and bays of the Whulge. Each night they camped at a new place. When they had gathered and preserved enough shellfish for winter, they returned to their village on Bainbridge Island.

On their second journey, the Squamish headed inland to the prairies and mountain slopes. There the women dug roots and picked berries while the men hunted. Through many seasons of hunting, Sealth's arms and legs grew strong and his aim sharpened. When his tribe had gathered a winter's supply of roots, berries, and game, they hauled it back to the Whulge.

At midsummer, Sealth's people would set out on their last and longest trip, to fish the rivers and lakes. Using the kelp line, bone hook, and clam bait, Sealth became an expert fisherman. When the Squamish returned home in early November, their winter food supply was overflowing.

After each trip the Squamish dried and stored away the food they had collected. Roots and berries were dried in

In midsummer the Squamish fished the rivers and lakes near the Whulge for salmon.

the sun. Some of the berries were mashed and pressed into cakes. The fish and meat were roasted beside huge fires and dried. Dried clams were put on strings.

Next, the food was wrapped in leaves and packed into reed baskets. The baskets were set on shelves along the walls of each house. In late November, the shelves were bulging with food. By the following May, they would be almost empty.

It may have been one November when the shelves were full that Schweabe noticed how cramped their houses were. The cooking fires filled them with smoke, and the dogs ran in and out of the tiny huts. Schweabe decided something must be done.

Around 1800, the Squamish began building a huge house

that would have room enough for all of their people. When finished, it would be strong enough to protect them from enemy attacks. They named it *Oleman* or "Old-Man-House." Schweabe hoped that other Whulge tribes might want to live there, too.

First, the Squamish had to find a place to build the huge house. Old-Man-House must have a sheltered cove, Schweabe told them, with good fishing nearby and a look-out spot. It took a year and a half to find the perfect site. They found it on the western mainland, a thousand feet across from the northwest corner of Bainbridge Island.

Agate Pass flowed between the island and the mainland, and the waterway was full of fish. The site had a commanding view of the Whulge. From it the Squamish could travel north or south with the coming and going of the tide.

Schweabe hoped Old-Man-House would help unite all the people of the sound. Banding together, he said, they would have plenty of food, warmth in winter, and protection from their enemies.

Sealth, who was now in his teens, helped in the great task of building Old-Man-House. It stretched nine hundred feet along the beach and covered as much ground as three city blocks. Seventy-four pillars, four feet wide and fifteen feet long, supported the thick cedar-slab roof. Inside the house were forty "apartments," room for all the Squamish and more.

It took years of hard work to build the giant house. A strong cedar door swung on a heavy post and was bolted by a log on the inside. It would keep them safe from the attacks of their northern enemies.

By the time Old-Man-House was finished, the handsome

Sealth was nearly twenty. Schweabe began to speak to him about marriage. He wanted Sealth to choose a Duwamish woman in hopes that it would make stronger ties between the two tribes. Schweabe had chosen his own wife, Scholitza, from the Duwamish.

The real name of Sealth's bride is a secret that has been lost in history. The Squamish never spoke the name of a loved one after their death for fear of disturbing their spirit. So at the time of her death, her name was forgotten. She is known to us as La Daila.

The proud Schweabe prepared for the wedding. For such special events as marriage, people of the Whulge gave a "potlatch." "Potlatch" means "gift-giving." The giver of the potlatch gathered up his most valuable possessions and simply gave them away to his guests. The gifts might be fish, furs, clothing, canoes, or any other prized item.

Later, land-taking whites found this openhanded giving hard to understand. To them it seemed foolish. But to the northwest Indians, it meant a lot more. The celebration of an important event, like a wedding, was a chance for the potlatch-giver to both show and share his wealth.

The more a person gave away to others, the more important he was in their society. Sharing one's wealth was a way of life. Food, clothing, and other needed goods moved freely from the hands of those who had too much into the hands of those who didn't have enough.

Schweabe and Sealth loaded up their gifts and canoed across the Whulge to give their wedding potlatch for the Duwamish. One of the canoes was a potlatch gift. It carried other gifts of food, blankets, shells, and beads. They were welcomed by the bride's father who spoke with favor of the

Everyone had a good time at the potlatch held for Sealth's wedding. It may have looked much like this modern day celebration.

marriage. After they had stayed a week, Schweabe and Sealth returned to Old-Man-House.

Several months later the Duwamish came to the Squamish village, and the wedding continued. The bride's father gave a return-potlatch for the Squamish with even more generous gifts. Following the gift-giving, the two tribes sang tribal songs and performed their dances for each other.

At last, the hands of Sealth and La Daila were joined. The bride's father presented the couple with a canoe for visits to the Duwamish village. In return, Schweabe invited a canoe-load of Duwamish to live at Old-Man-House. On the next day, La Daila was left with Sealth's people, and the Duwamish canoed home.

CHAPTER IV

Chief Sealth

The marriage of Sealth led to friendly union between the Squamish and Duwamish. Sealth was well thought of among the Duwamish, and La Daila was loved by Sealth's people. The tribal union started by their marriage was not at all like the union Schweabe had tried to force upon his neighbors.

From Sealth's youngest days, his father had told him that one day their people would rule the Duwamish. Schweabe had used force to try to bring about unity between the two tribes, and he had failed. Now Sealth would use friendship and cooperation. By marrying La Daila, he had already replaced bad tribal feelings with good ones.

The Squamish had been fighting the Chemacum to the the north and the Skokomish to the west, as the two tribes raided the edges of Squamish lands. The Duwamish, on the east, were less warlike. But Schweabe wanted their rich fishing grounds, and he had fought constantly to overcome them. As a result, many Duwamish had been killed.

Schweabe was a man of wars. Sealth was becoming a man of words. Talking to gain peace seemed a better way to him than fighting. Peace-talking could save much bloodshed, Sealth said. He would use talk to smooth the way for peace, and fight only if he was forced to.

And at first, Sealth was forced to fight. Northern tribes hammered away at the Squamish with constant surprise attacks. The tatoo-covered raiders swept down the sound in seventy-foot war canoes. Hundreds of warriors leaped from the boats, killing and carrying off women and children for slaves.

Old-Man-House provided some protection from attacks. When the Haida, Tlingit, and Tsimshian swooped down from the north, the Squamish ran inside their strong house. There arrows found their marks less easily. Still, though there was less killing and fewer slaves carried off, the raids went on.

The Squamish now looked to Sealth, as well as Schweabe, to lead them. The young peacemaker decided that they must fight if they were to have peace. The northern tribes must be taught a lesson.

Schweabe supported his son's decision to fight. Kitsap, the war chief, prepared to lead the attack, and the Squamish carved out new war canoes.

Sealth invited the Duwamish to join the war party. They must unite or be killed, he told them. With his powerful voice and his stirring words, he won their support.

The two tribes put together a swift fleet of two hundred canoes. Squamish and Duwamish women prepared food for the trip: clams, dried roots, and pemmican, pounded cakes of lean meat.

As the warriors moved northward, their war chants rang out along the Whulge. The beating clack of paddles broke in on the sad tribal song. From both shores of the sound, women's voices answered the song with one of their own.

Old-Man-House helped to protect Sealth's people from attacks by northern tribes in swift war canoes.

Young Sealth had put new hope in their hearts. If the war party was successful, they would be free from the cruelty of northern enemies.

The raiders loosed the first attack against the Nootka at Vancouver Island, seventy-five miles north. The Nootka were stunned by the unexpected raid. The fierce enemies of the north found out that the Whulge tribes could make war —and win!

And win they did, in surprise after surprise upon their enemies. From Vancouver Island, they sailed for Cape Flattery and raided other northern tribes. They set fire to the cedar stockades and threw burning mats over the walls. The harsh howl of their war cry echoed through camp after camp.

From village to village, the booty piled up in the raiders' canoes. There were blankets of mountain goat wool, bladders of whale and seal oil, and long strings of *hiaqua* shells, the "money" of the north. Most prized of all were the Haida canoes they captured. The huge, gently-curved boats glided swiftly over the water.

When the raiders came back to the Whulge, the two tribes celebrated their many victories. Their plunder was rich. But more valuable by far than all they took was the new peace they now enjoyed. Surprise raids from the north lessened and finally stopped.

The tribes of the north were not the only ones who attacked the people of the Whulge. From time to time, Indians from the east also attacked the coastal tribes. One of these attacks led Sealth to become the leader of the allied tribes of Puget Sound.

One day Sealth's brother-in-law paddled at full speed

Sealth led the united tribes in raids against their northern enemies. The warriors may have attacked a Haida village much like this one.

across the Whulge from the Duwamish camp. He brought warning of an attack by the Muckleshoots and other tribes from the upper White and Green rivers.

Under Kitsap's direction, Sealth's forces made ready for battle once more. Heartened by the bold victories of the Squamish and Duwamish, four other Whulge tribes joined in the union.

The six tribes held a council of war. Kitsap said they could outwit the attackers by hiding in the forest. Schweabe said that they should bring all the people into Old-Man-House for safety. There were many arguments over what to do because the six tribes had never worked together before.

After the older leaders had had their say, the tribes chose the ambush plan of a young man—Sealth. His deep, commanding voice rallied both young and old around him. The six tribes, who had fought often among themselves, now united for battle. They chose Sealth to lead the attack.

Next morning at daybreak, Sealth led his warriors to a sharp bend on the White River where the raiding party was sure to pass. On the river bank they put Sealth's plan into action. With stone axes and wedges, they chopped away at a giant fir. After hours of work, the tree fell across the river. It rested just above the water.

The attackers wouldn't see it until they reached the bend. Then it would be too late. The current would fling their canoes against the tree. Sealth's ambush party hid behind the banks with bows and arrows ready. At dusk, five enemy canoes with a hundred warriors neared the river bend.

Before the shocked raiders could stop, three of their canoes had smashed into the fallen tree. Sealth's troops sprang up on the banks and let fly a swarm of arrows. Most of the attackers were killed. The two rear canoes were warned, and some of their rowers barely escaped with their lives.

A victory celebration was held at Old-Man-House. In a grand council of the six tribes, Sealth was chosen as leader of the new tribal union.

For Sealth, now in his early twenties, it was his last feat of war. The cost of the peace he had won between Indian tribes had been high. In this moment of glory, he could not know how much higher the cost of peace between his people and white people would be.

CHAPTER V

Sealth the Peacemaker

Around 1810 Sealth became the leader of the allied tribes. The next ten years were happy ones for him. To settle conflicts and keep the peace, he spent much time traveling among his people. Coming home to La Daila was a peaceful pause from the cares of leadership.

When Sealth was told that he would soon be a father, his joy overflowed! One warm spring day, Sealth's wife gave birth to a daughter. The proud parents named their child Kickisomlo.

But their joy was cut short when the young mother fell sick after the birth. Day by day her strength slipped away. Every known medicine was given to her, but she did not get any better.

Sealth watched beside her bed, silently suffering the pain of his grief. When she died, he felt the loss deeply. Gone was the comfort her love had given to him.

In the custom of the Squamish, the body of Sealth's wife was wrapped in skins and laid in a canoe on the limbs of a tall tree. It was pointed toward the setting sun to light her way. Her name was quickly forgotten so that her spirit would find rest. But her love would always be remembered by Sealth.

27 SEALTH THE PEACEMAKER

The years after his wife's death were a sad time in the life of the Squamish chief. Trying to escape his sorrow, Sealth wandered around the Whulge. At times he sought relief in quiet places. At other times he went from village to village, seeking comfort in the tribal games played among his people. Win or lose, the hurt of his loss drove him on.

During these years, Sealth's growing daughter was good company for him each time he returned to Old-Man-House. Chubby Kickisomlo was a sweet yet sad reminder of La Daila. Soon after each return, he would be off again. When her father was away, the wild "Weewick," as she was known, ruled the Squamish camp. No one except her "Great Papa" could control her.

In time Sealth married a woman named Oiahl, and in later years he would enjoy the five children born to them. But during these sad years, he took little delight in his new family. Sealth kept on the move.

The white settlers were on the move, too. In 1805, Lewis and Clark, the American explorers, had established an overland route to the Pacific Ocean. In the years that followed, whites began to settle along the Columbia River to the south, though none had yet come to Squamish lands. In 1833 the Hudson's Bay Company of Canada established the first white settlement on Puget Sound, a trading post at Nisqually.

Eager to trade, Sealth took a bundle of his best beaver skins and paddled south to the new settlement. But he was disappointed in what he found. The white traders spoke only Chinook, an Indian-white trading language which Sealth could not yet understand. They demanded more furs in trade from him than from other Indians who lived nearby.

When one of Sealth's old enemies taunted him about being cheated, Sealth scuffled with him and left the settlement.

Among the first white people to arrive at Puget Sound were the Catholic missionaries. The first missionary Sealth met was Father Demers. Demers was a big man called "Sampson" by the other priests. Sealth respected him and called him the "Great Good Chief." He spread the word among his people to come and hear the big man who taught a big idea. Indians from all over the Whulge came to hear the spellbinding Bible stories told so well by Father Demers.

The priest told the Indians to worship. The Indians were puzzled. Hadn't they always worshipped the gods of their ancestors? They were told that murder was wrong. They had thought of it simply as a way to pay back wrongs done to them. When Father Demers told them how God loved his son, Jesus, Sealth could recall his own father's love.

Though Sealth was puzzled by some things, he understood others, and he decided to become a Christian. He was baptized along with many of his people. Sealth became more a peacemaker than ever. Morning and evening prayers were made a part of tribal life. Sealth told his people that stealing, fighting, and murder are wrong. The Great Spirit meant for all people to love one another.

But Sealth's new-found faith in brotherhood was soon to be tested. Clashes between white settlers and American Indians were nearing the peaceful shores of the Whulge.

Eastward across the Cascades, land-hungry whites were taking Indian lands. To the southeast, the Klickitats were roused to war by the many white settlers moving in around them. And to the northeast, Chief Patkanim of the Snoqualmi called together eight thousand Indians from around

Catholic missionaries in the Pacific Northwest started schools for Indian students. This photo, taken in 1865, shows Indian children at a Catholic school in the Puget Sound area.

the Whulge and urged them to war. Sealth's people were asked to join the battle.

Sealth urged the Indians toward the path of peace just as strongly as Patkanim urged them to war. Patkanim refused to listen to Sealth. He led his followers to war and was defeated. As a result of that battle, the white army built Fort Steilacoom, the first fort on Puget Sound, in 1850. The battle lines were drawn!

Fort Steilacoom was built to protect the white settlers who were taking the land of the Indians.

The Squamish and most other Whulge Indians did not draw near the battle lines. Except for a few small bands, the allied tribes would never join the battle against whites. Because of Chief Sealth, they did not fear the coming of the white settlers. Soon they would welcome them to the Whulge.

CHAPTER VI

The Bostons Arrive

Sealth was in his sixties by the time the first white settlers came to the land of his people. He had known for some time that they would come. Reports of white settlement had reached him at Old-Man-House. They told of trouble caused by white settlers taking the land of other Northwest tribes.

Because of his respect for the white world, Sealth had decided to make peace with the white settlers when they came to his land. The first of those settlers came from the city of Boston. So the people of the Whulge called the whites "Bostons."

The first Bostons had come across the United States in covered wagons in 1851 over the Oregon Trail. Leaving their wagons and families at Portland, in the Oregon Territory, the Boston men headed north toward Puget Sound. After a stop at Nisqually, they moved up the Duwamish River and settled on Duwamish land.

Some of these Bostons moved further up the Duwamish River to the Whulge. In September 1851, John Low, Lee Terry, and David Denny settled at Alki Point, right across the sound from Old-Man-House. Sealth greeted the pioneers with a friendly handshake.

The first Bostons made the long, difficult journey across the United States over the Oregon Trail.

THE BOSTONS ARRIVE

Using sign language, David Denny asked the chief for a canoe to explore the land further. Sealth gave him a canoe and two guides as well. He hoped they would stay.

The other two Bostons staked out a cabin site. The Squamish watched as the whites struggled to build the cabin. Several days later, one of the Bostons went to Portland to bring up their families.

When Lee Terry left for Nisqually to get a log splitter, David Denny was left alone to work on the cabin. The Squamish watched the lone white. While he was working on the cabin, the axe slipped and cut deep into his foot. Sick with fever, the young Denny kept working. Chills shook his body, and skunks stole his food. But still he worked. The Squamish admired his courage.

Sealth was about to offer help when the *Exact* arrived at Alki Point on November 13, 1851. The *Exact* was a small salmon boat, piloted by Captain Robert Fay. It carried the Boston families from Portland. Out of its tiny hold climbed twelve adults and just as many children belonging to the five families.

The Squamish watched as the Bostons lugged boxes and barrels from the ship. Soon the *Exact* left. The Bostons had come to stay. They were a young group—only two were over thirty. The Squamish were fascinated by the women's sunbonnets, which looked like huge clamshells, and by the Boston children, whose skin looked extra white.

David Denny introduced the newcomers to Sealth. The Squamish chief welcomed them to the green land, saying they would live together as friends. The whites couldn't understand his words, but his friendliness was clear even to the youngest Boston.

For many of those who had just come from Portland, Sealth's welcome was the only hint of friendliness they had known in this strange land. They were weary from the long, westward journey and the cramped sea voyage. Now here was this lonely, rainy place where they must live in one roofless cabin among people so unlike themselves. It all looked terribly bleak. Some of the new arrivals wept.

Sealth quickly offered help. The Squamish taught the Bostons to split thick cedar logs and to make huge slabs for cabin walls instead of the small logs they had used. It wasn't long before two cabins stood on Alki Point. The Squamish also showed their white friends how to fish the Whulge and the rivers, where to dig clams, and which plants of the woods and fields to use.

From the Squamish, the Bostons learned to strip cedar bark and to make rope, baskets, and many other things they needed. When the milk supply ran out, the Indian women brought clam juice for the Boston babies. With the help of Sealth's people, the Bostons survived the long, harsh winter of 1851-52.

Sealth believed that his people and the Bostons could

Sealth's people taught the Bostons how to live in their strange new home.

help each other. The Squamish taught the Bostons how to live in their strange new home. In return, the Bostons and their guns gave protection to the Squamish. During that winter no attacks came from their enemies to the north.

More than a thousand people from Sealth's allied tribes moved onto Alki Point. They placed their tent-like huts close by the settlers' cabins.

Sealth's people trusted the Bostons, but the Bostons did not trust them in return. They called the Indians "savages," as most whites did. They looked down upon the Indians and thought of themselves as better.

The prideful Bostons found it hard to live with their Indian neighbors. They didn't like the Indian custom of coming into their cabins without knocking. And their anger flared when the Indians took things without asking. For thousands of years, the world had been free for the Indians to enter and take. They saw nothing wrong with taking what they needed. After all, they gave freely to the Bostons.

Sealth had to tell his people that the Bostons didn't share things in the way the Indians were used to. They must learn the white people's ways, he said, so that Indians and whites could live together in peace. So the Indians changed some of their ways, but the Bostons would not change any of theirs to try to live in peace with their neighbors.

Not all Indians welcomed the coming of the Bostons to Puget Sound. Green River tribes to the east didn't want the whites settling on Indian lands. They were angry at Sealth's people for making friends with them.

During the cold, rainy winter of 1851-52, Sealth received an urgent message from Old-Man-House. His wife Oiahl was sick. He set out quickly to bring her across the Whulge to Alki Point. While he was gone, a small band of Green River warriors came to the Alki Point settlement. They carried muskets and their faces were filled with anger.

The fearful Bostons watched from their cabins. John Kanim and other Alki Point Indians lined up in front of the scowling band. Both sides glared at each other. Just when it looked like a fight would break out, the Green River Indians turned and left as quickly as they had come.

When Sealth returned and heard what had taken place, he called his people together. He told them that they must not fight. But neighboring tribes were growing more and more bitter, and the threat of war was not far away.

That winter Oiahl died. Her death made Sealth think about bringing a white doctor to Alki Point.

Sealth had been impressed by the skill of white missionary doctors. He had met Dr. David Maynard while trading at Olympia. Maynard ran a trading post at that village on the south edge of Puget Sound. The Indians trusted the good-natured doctor, and he dealt fairly with them. In the grip of that bad winter, Sealth decided to ask Maynard to come to Alki Point.

CHAPTER VII

Seattle

Late in the winter of 1852, Sealth canoed down the Whulge to Olympia. He had traded many furs at Maynard's trading post. Always the trades had been fair. Sealth knew that if the doctor would come with him, his people would have good trading and good medicine as well.

Of all the white people Sealth had met, jolly Dr. Maynard was his favorite. When he was with the doctor, somehow he forgot that the worlds of Indian and white were two different worlds. They had shared many good times, and a warm friendship had grown up between them.

David Maynard had come west from Ohio in 1850, bringing only his doctor's bag. From the moment he opened his store in Olympia, Maynard was known for treating Indians with fairness.

No wonder Sealth thought Maynard was just the person the Alki Point settlement needed. He found the easy-going storekeeper ready to move. Some people at Olympia said that the owners of rival stores had asked Maynard to leave. He sold his goods at low prices, they complained, and often gave them away to poor Indians and whites. Still he was successful.

Sealth told the doctor how much he was needed at Alki

David Maynard respected the Indian way of life and treated the people fairly. He and Sealth became lifelong friends.

Point. Maynard said he would go. As soon as his goods were loaded, they set off up the Whulge. On the last day of March 1852, they landed at Alki Point, now called "New York" by the settlers.

Maynard told Sealth that New York was not a good place for a trading post. The water was too shallow for trading ships, he said. And there was no protection from the wind.

Sealth led the doctor around Alki Point and eastward along the beach into Elliott Bay. Nestled deep inside the bay was an eight-acre island of Duwamish land—one of Sealth's choicest campgrounds. Across from it, the mainland rose high above the water. The chief had been carefully saving that spot. Now he offered it freely to Maynard to use as he needed—not to take for all time. In doing so, Sealth acted according to an honored tradition of his people.

He was sharing his wealth with other people in need.

The doctor liked the spot. In the middle of the waterfront was a steep bank three hundred feet long. Safe from the ups and downs of the tide, it would be perfect for shipping. Along the shore there was a mile-long flat, muddy beach where the Indians could land their canoes easily.

Using the few Squamish words he knew, Maynard told Sealth his plans. By the time his trading post opened, he would be speaking their language well.

While Sealth was bringing Maynard from Olympia, the Alki Point settlers had dragged the harbor at Elliott Bay with a horseshoe on a rope. They agreed that it was a much better location. That spring, most of them moved over from New York and took claims on Sealth's land-gift along Elliott Bay. Soon a tiny village was growing there.

The Indians moved to the island campground off the point, now called Maynard's Point. They traded their salmon, berries, clams, and goose feathers for molasses, coffee, axes, and bright-colored cloth at the doctor's new store. Also, they cut timber which he shipped to San Francisco. Because of the fair and thriving trade, both Sealth's people and the doctor enjoyed a new-found wealth.

Maynard's trading post was a huge success. Arthur Denny opened a store that sold groceries, hardware, and clothes. The Indians traded their fish and furs at the doctor's post and spent their earnings for the goods at the store. They also dug potatoes and served as guides for the settlers. The peaceful village was growing rapidly.

Soon a new face appeared behind the counter of the trading post. It was Catherine Maynard, Dr. Maynard's new wife. The Indians quickly grew fond of her. Catherine and Sealth's daughter, Kickisomlo, were the same age and became close friends. The Maynards were leaders of the fast-growing white settlement. David Maynard was not only doctor and merchant to the village, but also logger, land-seller, lawyer, and justice of the peace.

Sealth was the leader of the Indian members of the new settlement. Their island campground was logged off and made larger. At first a bridge had been built between the island and the mainland. When ships from San Francisco dumped their ballast of dirt and rocks at the edges of the island, the new land fill caused the island to grow out and join the mainland. Soon the bridge was no longer needed.

So far the village had no name. Giving it a name almost destroyed the friendship between the chief and the doctor. The village was still in the Oregon Territory. Because it was on Duwamish land, the Oregon lawmakers had given it the name "Duwamps." But most of the settlers didn't like that name.

Some of them wanted to call the village "London" or "Paris." But others, like Maynard, thought it should have an Indian name, since the Indians had helped so much in building it. More Indians than whites lived in the village, and the Indians had given them the land on which it was built.

One day a group of settlers suggested naming it "Sealth." Others said that the name was too hard to say. Only an Indian could say it right, they argued. And it was true. "Sealth" is one of several English spellings for the name, which is difficult to pronounce in our language. The ending of Sealth's name twisted every English-speaking tongue that tried to say it. Most of the Bostons agreed, however, that

Large sailing ships from San Francisco came to Seattle's new harbor.

it was a good idea to name the village after him. He had helped them more than anyone.

So it happened. "Sealth" was changed to "Seattle." "Seattle" was smoother and easier to say. In May 1853, the Oregon lawmakers gave in and changed the name of the village to "Seattle." The settlers expected Sealth to feel honored that their village had been named after him. But they had forgotten a very important Squamish custom.

Sealth was very angry when he heard the news. They must not name the village after him, he said. If they did, whenever the name was spoken after his death, his spirit would be disturbed in the grave. But the whites did not understand. His name had been taken. And, like the Indian lands, it would not be given back.

Maynard and others tried to explain to Sealth that they

The fast-growing settlement was named "Seattle" in honor of Sealth.

were trying to honor him and meant no harm. When they said the name "Seattle," they would be speaking of a village, not him. Sealth was still unhappy. For a long time he stayed away from Maynard's trading post.

When another harsh winter hit the Whulge in 1853-54, Sealth put aside his hurt. The white settlers ran out of food in the cold, snowy weather. It would be a long time before a supply ship would come from San Francisco. Sealth and other Indians canoed up the Duwamish River to the inland meadows. There they dug wappatoes and brought them back to the village. With the help of the Indians, the Bostons kept from starving that winter.

But worse problems were in store for Sealth and his people. Neighboring tribes raged at them for helping the land-grabbing whites. Chiefs of tribes outside the Whulge complained to Sealth. The white people got everything, they told him. And when the whites got tired of the Indians, they said, the Indians would be kicked out like dogs.

There was truth in what the outsiders were saying. Already the Bostons had punished Indians for crimes against other Indians. Many of Sealth's own people believed the whites should not interfere. But Chief Sealth agreed with the whites. At that, the other chiefs accused him of turning his back on the Indians.

Sealth was deeply troubled. For days he wandered along the shores of the Whulge. Was he turning his back on his people? Was it wrong to help the white people?

Sealth would go on helping the whites. He would be true to his own people, too. But living in the white world and the Indian world at the same time was getting harder and harder. Sealth was the bridge between two worlds. That bridge would be strained almost to the breaking point.

CHAPTER VIII

Day and Night Cannot Dwell Together

A thousand people from Sealth's allied tribes stood along the beach in front of Dr. Maynard's trading post. They were waiting for the new white chief to arrive. Isaac Stevens had been appointed governor of the Washington Territory when it was formed in 1853.

As the Indians watched for the governor's ship, they must have been worried. White settlers in the Northwest were rapidly closing in around them. With more settlers came more white chiefs. Too many changes were coming too fast.

But the changes would come even faster when the new governor arrived. Stevens had worked for the railroads. Now, as governor, it was his job to find a route for the new Northern Pacific Railway over the Cascade Mountains into Puget Sound.

Stevens believed that the Indian people must be removed so that the land could be opened to white settlers. He had little respect for Indian rights to the land. Dashing from tribe to tribe, he was trying to get the Indians to sign away their land in treaties.

At last he arrived at Seattle. As soon as he set foot on the shore, he began speaking.

The new governor wanted to move Sealth's people from their lands.

"The Great Chief in Washington loves Indians," said Stevens hastily. "He wants to care for and protect you. He will buy your lands and move you to a place of your own." He chose his words carefully to hide the white plan to take Indian lands.

Stevens left little time for the interpreters to translate what he was saying for the Indians. Most of them could not understand what he was talking about. Before they knew it, the governor was finished.

Chief Sealth answered for his people. He understood what the crafty white man was saying, and there was more than a little scorn in his reply.

> The White Chief says that Big Chief at Washington sends us greetings of friendship and good will. This is kind of him for we know he has little need of our

friendship in return. His people are many. They are like the grass that covers great prairies. My people are few. They resemble the scattering trees of a storm-swept plain. The Great—and I presume—good White Chief sends us word that he wishes to buy our lands but is willing to allow us enough to live comfortably. This indeed appears just, even generous, for the Red Man no longer has rights that he need respect . . .

To us the ashes of our ancestors are sacred and their resting place is hallowed ground. You wander far from the graves of your ancestors and seemingly without regret. . . Our religion is the traditions of our ancestors—the dreams of our old men, given them in the solemn hours of night by the Great Spirit; and the visions of our sachems, and is written in the hearts of our people . . . .

Day and night can not dwell together. The Red Man has ever fled the approach of the White Man as the morning mist flees before the rising sun. . . .

Tribe follows tribe, and nation follows nation, like the waves of the sea. It is the order of nature, and regret is useless. Your time of decay may be distant—but it will surely come, for even the White Man whose God walked and talked with him as friend with friend, can not [escape] the common destiny. We may be brothers after all. We will see.

The governor's offer left little choice for the Indians. Sealth knew there was nothing his people could do to keep the whites from taking their land. So, with honor, he agreed to sign the treaty.

After shaking hands with the governor, Sealth left. His

longtime dream of Indians and whites sharing the land had been shattered. The white leader was set on removing the Indians. Sealth knew that it was useless to fight. The Indians had never won a war with the whites.

Stevens hurried off to more meetings with other Puget Sound tribes. He stumped north through Indian lands of the upper Whulge. Then he headed south to the land of the Nisqually and Puyallup. There he clashed with the two tribes when he tried to force them into a treaty on Christmas Day, 1854.

The Nisqually chief, Leschi, was angry. The white people were taking all the good land, he said, and leaving only the rocky hillside for the Indians. Leschi's people were farmers and needed the flat land. Stevens' answer was harsh: Take that land or none!

Leschi would not back down. He and many others were ready to fight for their land. All around the sound, Stevens' hasty actions were stirring up Indian anger.

Claycum, the Duwamish war chief, told Sealth that Indians all around them were ready to go to war. Sealth told him that fighting would do no good. He had given his word. He would sign the treaty.

In January 1855, Governor Stevens rushed back to sign the treaty with Sealth's allied tribes. Twenty-three hundred people from more than a dozen Whulge tribes came to Point Elliott for the treaty-signing.

Stevens spoke first. He told the Indians that he and their leaders would sign their names to the paper. Then it would be sent to the president in Washington, D.C. If he said it was good, it would stand forever.

The treaty was read and translated into Indian words.

Angered by the way the whites were taking Indian lands, Leschi called for the tribes to band together to fight the invaders.

But the paper was a mystery to most of the Indians. Only their leaders understood that they were giving up 99 percent of their land, and that they would be crowded into the 1 percent that was left. In return, the whites promised to pay the Indians a mere seven and a half cents an acre. The promise was not kept until four years later, and the Indians never received full payment.

Chief Sealth presented a white flag of peace to Governor Stevens. Then he spoke for his people. He said that he wished to put away all bad feelings so that Indians and whites could live in peace.

But all bad feelings were not put away. Governor Stevens turned eastward to remove the rest of the Indians from the Washington Territory. However, the Indians to the east were determined to fight. They wanted no part of Stevens' hasty treaties.

At Seattle, Sealth heard reports of attacks and counterattacks between Indians and whites to the east. Time after time, the warring Indians urged Sealth to join them. Each time he refused, but it caused a struggle within him. Was he being faithful to his own people?

Then came the day when his own son told Sealth that some of his people were calling him a traitor! Deeply saddened, the aging chief left Seattle. It would never be home to him again. He went back to Old-Man-House. Sealth had tried to bring Indians and whites together to live in peace. Now he felt outcast from both worlds.

On one of Sealth's worst days, his old friend, Dr. Maynard, came looking for him. Maynard had been appointed Indian agent for the reservation which was to be at Port Madison, near Old-Man-House. Sealth's people had not

Sealth was deeply saddened by the fighting between Indians and whites.

yet moved there. Maynard asked the chief to bring his people to the reservation. They must move the peaceful Indians away from those who made war, said the doctor.

Sealth agreed. They had to protect the Indians who had not gone to war. Perhaps they could live in peace in a land for Indians only around Old-Man-House. Maynard and Sealth worked as a team once again. Together, they moved more than a thousand people from Seattle to the reservation at Port Madison.

In December 1855, the United States sent the warship *Decatur* to Puget Sound to protect white settlers. There were killings and return-killings as the fighting grew into war. At Old-Man-House, Sealth watched with eyes grown sad and old as he heard each new report of violence.

CHAPTER IX

War

When a U.S. Army officer was killed near Seattle, the white settlers feared that the Indians would attack the village next. Lieutenant W. S. Slaughter was leading his troops in pursuit of a group of Indians through Naches Pass on December 3, 1855. In a surprise attack, Slaughter and several of his men were killed by the Indians they had been chasing.

Slaughter's body was carried down the Whulge by the warship *Decatur* to be buried at Fort Steilacoom. On the *Decatur's* return trip, the ship rammed against a rock in the Whulge. It caved in the ship's left side up to the water line, but it was able to make it back to Seattle where it was beached. With the warship crippled, the warring tribes saw their chance to attack. Led by Chief Leschi and Owhi, chief of the Klickitats, the warriors moved toward the village.

The crew of the *Decatur* repaired the ship quickly. Before the Indians could attack, the warship floated in Elliott Bay, and once again its guns protected Seattle. The Indian attack was delayed. But Leschi and Owhi were determined to attack the first chance they had.

At Old-Man-House, Sealth's scouts reported that some

As war grew near, the Decatur *was sent to protect the white settlers of Seattle from attack.*

Klickitats planned to kill the Maynards. Sealth had his warriors drive out all Klickitats from the Port Madison reservation. He showed the doctor and his wife how to dye their faces with berry juice, and Kickisomlo brought Squamish clothes to disguise Catherine. Sealth and his daughter led their two friends deep into the forest to make sure they were safe.

Before long a Duwamish scout reported that Leschi's warriors were only a few miles from Seattle. Sealth wanted to warn the people of the village, both Indians and whites. But he was past seventy now, and Dr. Maynard had been treating him for rheumatism. They decided that the doctor should go to warn the captain of the *Decatur* about Leschi's upcoming attack.

Maynard pushed off bravely in a canoe across the storm-

53 WAR

whipped Whulge. Sealth returned to guard Catherine Maynard's hideout. He watched and listened uneasily through the night.

At sunrise the Indian war cry rang out over the Whulge. The guns of the *Decatur* boomed in response—the battle was on!

Dr. Maynard returned just as the battle began. The settlers had been warned, he told Sealth. All work stopped at Port Madison while the tense Indians waited. Some of them snatched up what weapons they had and headed for canoes to join the fight. Sealth stopped them. He, too, feared for the lives of the Indians camped at Seattle, and for their white friends there. But they must follow the way of peace, he told them, and hope for the best.

Across the sound, the battle raged all day. Long after dark, the gunshots and war cries stopped.

In the morning the Whulge was hidden by thick fog. The guns of war were still silent. A group of Indians arrived from the village with the first news of the battle. The *Decatur* was still in Elliott Bay, they said. There had been much bloodshed, and Leschi's warriors had fled. There would be more fighting.

That night, Maynard gathered the Indians around the campfire to report on the battle. The settlers had withstood the attack, he told them. They would build a new blockhouse and fortify the village. It seemed certain they would win.

Leschi had left, the doctor said. But he had vowed to return before long to destroy Seattle. The rest of the Indians at the village must be brought to the reservation to protect them. Maynard asked Sealth's people to help. To-

All day long the battle raged, and the big guns of the warship boomed out over the harbor.

gether they brought many more people to Port Madison.

So the settlers were winning the war. But it was not only Leschi's followers who would be losers. All the Indian people of the Northwest would lose as well. They were losing their land, and living on that land was the only way they knew how to live.

The Indians were no longer free to live the way they had for centuries before the white settlers came. For them the tiny reservations were prisons. Shutting them up there would bring an end to their way of life. Sealth had tried the way of peace with the whites. Leschi had tried the way of war. Both men had lost.

CHAPTER X

A Change of Worlds

Four years dragged slowly by before the treaty with Chief Sealth's people was approved by the president and Congress. They were years of struggle for the Squamish. Cut off from their old way of life, they could no longer go on their yearly food-gathering journeys inland to the meadows and mountains. The whites took over more and more of their fishing grounds. In winter they had little to eat.

Sealth stood between his people and the whites. He told the white leaders that his people needed to be paid for their lands so they could survive. They had given up their lands to the settlers, but they had received nothing in return.

Leschi had fled to central Washington after the Battle of Seattle. There in the land of the Yakimas, it took almost a year for the white army to track him down. Leschi met with the white soldiers, and he promised to give up fighting and to live in peace.

When he returned to his homeland, he found his horses and land gone and a reward offered for him by Governor Stevens. Leschi was put on trial for the murder of a white man, but the jury found Leschi innocent of the charges made against him.

Five months later, Leschi was tried again. Sealth appealed to the governor to save Leschi. Could a leader be blamed for trying to keep his people from starving? he asked.

But Leschi was blamed, and he was sentenced to death. On February 19, 1858, Leschi was hanged for a murder that few people seemed sure he had committed.

Many of Sealth's people were saying that Leschi had been right not to trust the whites. Sealth continued to ask Governor Stevens to honor the treaty he had made with the allied tribes. Three years had passed, and still the U.S. Congress had not approved their treaty. The money promised for their land had not been sent. Where is our treaty? the people asked their chief. Sealth asked Dr. Maynard the same question.

After serving as Indian agents for two years, David and Catherine Maynard left Port Madison. They had given much of their own money to help Sealth's people. And they had given of themselves until their health began to fail. With sadness, Sealth watched them move back across the sound. They traded their land at Seattle for three hundred acres at Alki Point. There they farmed the land and served both Indian and white people.

The new Indian agent offered little treaty hope to Sealth. Just be patient, he told the chief. But Sealth had been patient. Now he grew more discouraged as the years passed and their treaty was not approved. His people had received only a few trinkets. The Squamish were not the strong tribe they once had been.

After four years of waiting, the treaty was finally approved on April 11, 1859. Still, no money was granted to the Indians. More lean years followed for Sealth's people.

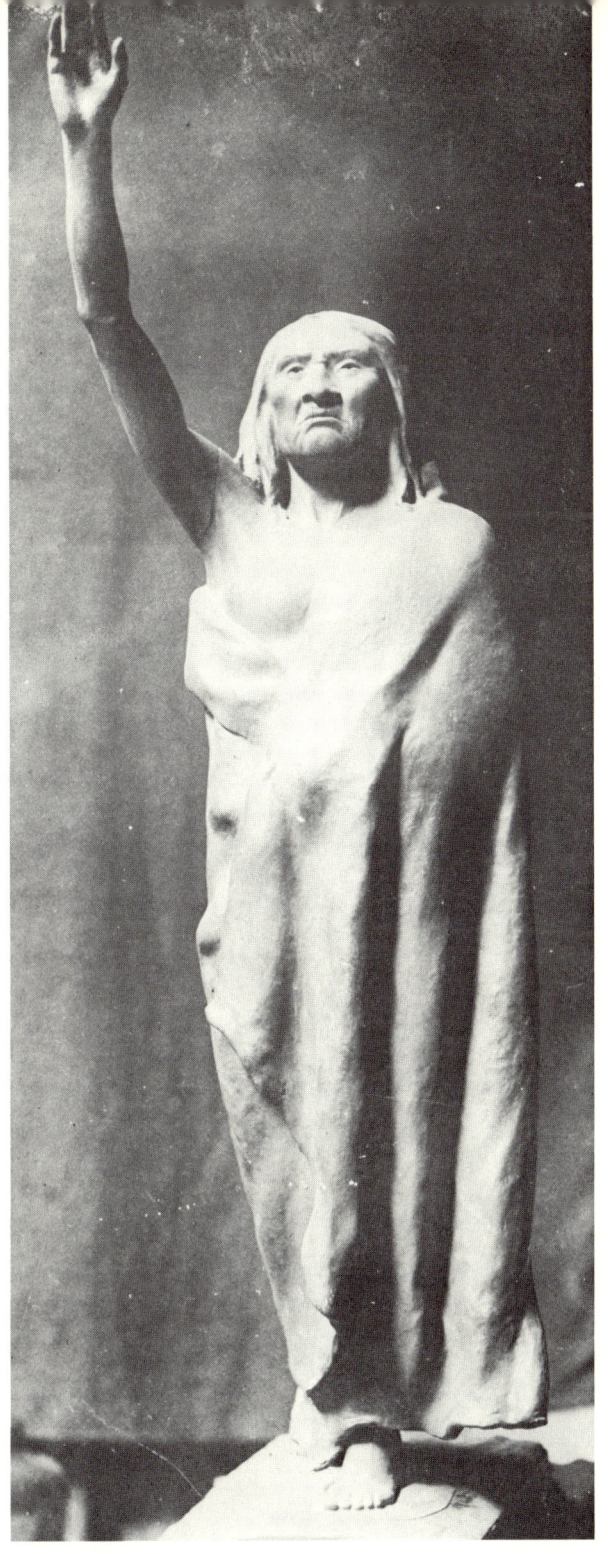

The people of Seattle built a statue to honor Chief Sealth.

During those years, the chief seldom visited Seattle. He no longer felt at home among the whites, and his illness made travel difficult.

Early in 1866, Sealth made his last trip across the Whulge. He sought out his old friends, the Maynards, and David and Catherine welcomed him. The doctor treated Sealth's sick body, but there was little he could do. A week later Sealth returned to Old-Man-House.

On June 7 he died. Hundreds of people, both Indian and white, came for Sealth's funeral. A Squamish sub-chief offered the Indians' praise for the great leader: "He knew better what was good for us than we knew ourselves." Across the Whulge in the city named for him, stands a statue of Sealth. It was the first statue built by the city of Seattle.

Sealth had done his best to unite the Indian and white worlds. He had hoped that the differences which kept them apart would slowly pass away. But those differences have been too great for Indians and whites to share the land in peace. In recent years the United Indians of All Tribes has sought to regain the land and fishing rights of their ancestors. Like the allied tribes who had once come together under Chief Sealth, they are American Indians living in the Puget Sound region.

One hundred years after his death, all of us have something to learn from Sealth. At the Spokane World's Fair, Expo '74, his thoughts about the oneness of life and the earth greeted visitors entering the United States pavilion: "The earth does not belong to man. Man belongs to the earth."

THE AUTHOR

Mel Boring is a freelance writer of stories and articles for children's magazines. *Sealth, the Story of an American Indian,* is his first published book. As a former elementary and junior high school teacher in Michigan and California, he has worked with young students for several years.

Mr. Boring has written many articles for children's magazines, and from 1973 to 1975 he wrote and edited audio-visual mathematics and metrics programs. A graduate of Sterling College in Kansas, he now lives in Vermont with his wife and two children.

NOTE ON THE TEXT:

The name of Sealth's people has been spelled in various ways to translate the name into the English alphabet. To make the name easy for young students to pronounce, the spelling "Squamish" rather than "Suquamish" or "Suquampsh" has been used in this book.

OTHER BIOGRAPHIES
IN THIS SERIES ARE

William Beltz
Robert Bennett
Black Hawk
Crazy Horse
Charles Eastman
Geronimo
Oscar Howe
Ishi
Pauline Johnson
Chief Joseph
Little Turtle
Maria Martinez
George Morrison
Daisy Hooee Nampeyo
Michael Naranjo
Osceola
Powhatan
Red Cloud
Will Rogers
John Ross
Sacagawea
Sequoyah
Sitting Bull
Maria Tallchief
Tecumseh
Jim Thorpe
Tomo-chi-chi
Pablita Velarde
William Warren
Annie Wauneka

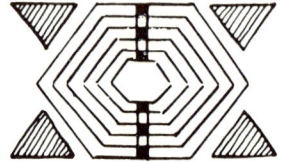

MTN. VIEW HIGH MEDIA CENTER